T0013679

The Book of Swagger

People, Places, and Things That Have
Swagger — And Some That Don't!

Ernie J. Zelinski

Visions International Publishing
P.O. Box 4072
Edmonton, Alberta, Canada, T6E 4S8
Phone: 780-434-9202   Email: vipbooks@telus.net

Distributed to Canadian bookstores by Sandhill Book Marketing, Unit #4 - 3308 Appaloosa Road, Kelowna, B.C., V1V 2W5 (info@sandhillbooks.com) and to US bookstores by National Book Network, 4501 Forbes Blvd., Ste. 200, Lanham, MD (Phone: 800-462-6420)

The Book of Swagger / Ernie J. Zelinski
ISBN 978-1-927452-07-3

Photo Credits
Greg Gazin: Page 69, Page 71, and Page 156
Gordon Drevor: Page 83
Michel Mazeau/ Wikimedia Commons: Page 155

Printed in Canada

Inspiration for High Achievers

"If you follow the crowd, you will likely get no further than the crowd. If you walk alone, you're likely to end up in places no one has ever been before. Being an achiever is not without its difficulties, for peculiarity breeds contempt. The unfortunate thing about being ahead of your time is that when people finally realize you were right, they'll simply say it was obvious to everyone all along. You have two choices in life. You can dissolve into the main stream, or you can choose to become an achiever and be distinct. To be distinct, you must be different. To be different, you must strive to be what no else but you can be."

— Alan Ashley-Pitt

Other Remarkable Books by Ernie J. Zelinski

The Lazy Person's Guide to Success — Financial Independence and Personal Freedom Too! (over 110,000 copies sold)

Look Ma, Life's Easy: How Ordinary People Attain Extraordinary Success and Remarkable Prosperity (published in 7 languages)

Life's Secret Handbook: Reminders for Adventurous Souls Who Want to Make a Big Difference in This World

Career Success Without a Real Job: The Career Book for People Too Smart to Work in Corporations (published in 5 languages)

The Lazy Person's Guide to Happiness: Shortcuts to a Happy and Fulfilling Life (over 80,000 copies sold and published in 5 languages)

101 Really Important Things You Already Know, But Keep Forgetting (over 50,000 copies sold and published in 10 languages)

The Joy of Being Retired: 365 Reasons Why Retirement Rocks — and Work Sucks!

The Joy of Not Working: A Book for the Retired, Unemployed and Overworked (over 310,000 copies sold and published in 17 languages)

How to Retire Happy, Wild, and Free: Retirement Wisdom You Won't Get from Your Financial Advisor (over 460,000 copies sold)

The Little Black Book of Swagger: 637 Swagger Tips for Super Achievers

Table of Contents

Introduction

Let's face it: A lot of people wish they had more Swagger but they won't admit it. This could be you. Justin Bieber desired Swagger so much that he actually hired a Swagger Coach for three years. Charlie Hoehn, a successful author, marketer, and entrepreneur, wrote a feature blog post about how his lack of Swagger kept him from achieving what he could have achieved if he had more Swagger.

What is Swagger? The *Merriam-Webster Dictionary* defines it as "An act or instance of swaggering. Arrogant or conceitedly self-assured behavior. Ostentatious display or bravado. A self-confident outlook. Cockiness." *Urban Dictionary*, on the other hand, has a more positive definition that gives Swagger a much better name. "Swagger is to move with confidence, sophistication, and to be cool. Swagger is to conduct yourself in a way that would automatically earn respect." For purposes of this book we will run with the *Urban Dictionary* meaning.

So what type of people have Swagger? Individuals who know how to live with flair have Swagger. They dress with Swagger; they travel to cities with Swagger; they eat at restaurants with Swagger; and they drive cars with Swagger. In this regard, Swagger is about good taste, which is ultimately good for you.

Swagger is also about great confidence. What about modesty? Renowned Harvard University economist John Kenneth Galbraith once pointed out, "Modesty is a vastly overrated virtue." In the same vein, former Israel Prime Minister Golda Meir advised, "Don't be humble. You're not that great." In other words, people who claim they are modest or humble normally have accomplished absolutely nothing to be modest or humble about.

Some people will protest that Swagger is all about ego. Of course, it is. Humbleness is all about ego too! So has every single post made on social media been all about ego. Furthermore, all the discoveries and positive advances for humanity have been the result of individual ego. For example, it was due to Steve Job's ego that the iPhone was developed and made such an impact on humanity.

Occasionally people will say to me, "Ernie, you have a big ego." My reply is, "Yes, I do. But I have never taken a selfie in my life and yet you are constantly taking selfies. Who has the bigger ego?" Fact is, individuals who claim to have little or no ego are on the biggest ego trip any human can be on.

Let's face it. Trying to please everyone and anyone is a fool's game at best. Attempting to dumb it down and average it out is not going to work at the best of times. Swagger is always and exclusively for the achiever who behaves differently.

Swagger is rising to the occasion when required. American General Creighton W. Abrams announced, "They've got us surrounded again, the poor bastards." In the same vein, British Royal Navy Officer Sir Andrew Cunningham proclaimed, "We are so outnumbered there's only one thing to do. We must attack." When faced with a crisis, leaders with Super Swagger listen to advice from the experts and then spectacularly ignore it. As the Russians started attacking his country, President V. Zelensky was offered passage out of the Ukraine for his safety. He refused. He proclaimed, "I need ammunition, not a ride." Now that's Swagger!

What about people who despise achievers with Swagger? No doubt in the republic of human mediocrity Swagger is despised. French Author and Nobel Prize winner André Gide advised, "It is better to be hated for what you are than to be loved for what you are not." If you have confidence in yourself and display this confidence with fabulous flair, the heck with what the haters of this world think! Debaters will debate, potatoes will potate, tomatoes will tomate, and haters will hate. Haters hate because that's the only thing they are good at. In response to the haters, super achievers with Swagger will swaggate.

According to *The Little Black Book of Swagger (637 Swagger Tips for Super Achievers)*, there are three types of Swagger: 1. Elegant Swagger, 2. Super Swagger, and 3. Raunchy Swagger. Actually, there is a fourth type — Evil Swagger. It's best to leave Evil Swagger for others to pursue.

Whatever the type, Swagger gives you intrigue, something the mediocre in society don't have. "It is cruel to discover one's mediocrity only when it is too late," warned British writer W. Somerset Maugham. Do you want to be mediocre? Of course, not. Languishing in painful obscurity for the rest of your life will not bring you joy and satisfaction. True Swagger will. Individuals with Swagger may not be able to tolerate a long succession of ordinary days but they are consistent in their pursuit of excellence, success, and extraordinary accomplishment in their field of work.

So can one develop Swagger? Giving up on ever having Swagger because you believe that you can't develop it is definitely not a Swagger move. Being too guarded and self-conscious does not translate into

Swagger. Any time someone can rise to the occasion with total fearlessness and overbearing confidence, that person is exhibiting true Swagger. Think Mick Jagger. Think Mohammad Ali. Think Nancy Pelosi. Think Denzel Washington. Think Jen Sincero. Think Cleopatra. Think Kevin O'Leary. Think Elizabeth Arden. We are talking about unwavering confidence.

Truth be known, Swagger makes the world much more interesting. Swagger abounds everywhere in this world. The Swagger lists in this book comprise various categories that may be about comedians, cynics, creeps, cowboys, and con artists. Possibly even about cars, cafés, coffee, celebrities, cities, cuisine, currencies, and countries.

Discovering the people, places, and things that have Swagger in the following pages may just help you develop some Swagger yourself. More Swagger will result in a more powerful individuality. When it comes, remember to embrace your Swagger even if the habitual haters and pathological critics don't.

Top 10 Cities in the World with the Most Swagger

1. New York, USA
2. Prague, Czechia
3. Paris, France
4. London, England
5. Rio de Janeiro, Brazil
6. Istanbul, Turkey
7. Sydney, Australia
8. Tokyo, Japan
9. Rome, Italy
10. Buenos Aires, Argentina

John Lennon loved New York and moved there because he thought it was the center of the art world but forgot to mention that New York also represents Swagger like no other city in the world.

Top 10 Cities in the US with the Most Swagger

1. New York, New York
2. Las Vegas, Nevada
3. San Francisco, California
4. New Orleans, Louisiana
5. Honolulu, Hawaii
6. Los Angeles, California
7. Chicago, Illinois
8. San Diego, California
9. Phoenix, Arizona
10. Boston, Massachusetts

Whoever with Swagger can go to New York — will go to New York!

Top 10 Reasons Why New York Has Swagger

1. It's the financial capital of the world.
2. With Broadway, New York is the world capital of theater.
3. Times Square, as Timothy F. Cahill said, makes you feel like you're in the capital of the world.
4. Late nights, bright lights, it's the city that never sleeps.
5. New Yorkers speak more than 800 languages.
6. The city's Lombardi's was the first Pizzeria to open in the US.
7. The Statue of Liberty is the shining symbol of America.
8. The city's Federal Reserve Bank holds the most gold stored in the world.
9. The city has the largest Jewish population outside of Israel, the largest Chinese population outside of Asia, and the largest Puerto Rican population of any city in the world.
10. One in every 38 people in the US lives in New York City.

Frank Sinatra sang "I want to be a part of it, New York, New York", because it's got Super Swagger.

Top 10 Reasons Why Las Vegas Has Swagger

1. It's not only an easy place to get married — also to get a divorce.
2. Wayne Newton has performed here for years and made it his home.
3. No other city is as capable of liberating money from suckers.
4. It isn't a real City; it's its own magical world.
5. Elvis Presley sang *Viva Las Vegas* for a reason.
6. It has many nicknames including Glitter Gulch and Entertainment Capital of the World.
7. You can do practically anything you want 24 hours a day.
8. The best restaurants are off the Strip where the locals dine.
9. Its population has multiplied by a factor of 30 since the 1940s — more than that of any other major American city.
10. Ever-grander casinos open each and every year while others fail.

Swagger in Las Vegas is easily lost when one loses
everything including one's shirt.

Top 10 Reasons Why San Francisco Has Swagger

1. The Golden Gate Bridge was constructed during the Great Depression because none of city's banks failed during that time.
2. Saulsalito, across the SF Bay, is where Otis Redding wrote "(Sittin' On) the Dock of the Bay."
3. San Francisco 49ers is one of the greatest NFL teams ever.
4. Walking up its steep hills keeps you in great shape.
5. A group of California sea lions lives at the Pier 39 Marina.
6. It's Chinatown with great food is the largest in North America.
7. Lombard Street is a more crooked street than any in your city.
8. Haight-Ashbury was home of the hippie movement.
9. The United Nations Charter was drafted and ratified here in 1945.
10. Its cable cars are the only National Historic Monument that moves.

If your home town had as many great songs written about it as San Francisco, it would have a lot of Swagger too.

Top 10 Reasons Why New Orleans Has Swagger

1. "The Big Easy" describes the easy-going way of life in the city.
2. It's the spiritual birthplace of Jazz.
3. Practically every day is Mardi Gras in New Orleans.
4. Getting lost in the French Quarter is like getting lost in Heaven if you are a jazz and/or blues fan.
5. It's the only US city where you can get Cajun in your soul.
6. "Even the sidewalks in New Orleans have personality."
7. Its cultural diversity, the food, the music, and the architecture.
8. The late night life is even better than that in New York.
9. Eating at chain restaurants is taboo for anyone with Swagger.
10. The motto of New Orleans is "let the good times roll."

New Orleans has Swagger of a different sort — the Cajun French-based flavor originally brought to Louisiana by the exiles from the French colony of Acadia.

Top 10 Reasons Why Honolulu Has Swagger

1. It isn't called Paradise for nothing.
2. Practically everyone who visits here wants to live here.
3. It has as a perfect climate as that of anywhere in the world.
4. It has the best surfing in the world — surfing was invented here.
5. Waikiki Beach is where salt really lowers your blood pressure.
6. Its state is the only U.S. state with two official languages.
7. The only royal palace in the US is in Honolulu.
8. The closest location on the mainland United States to Honolulu is the Point Arena Lighthouse in California — 2,353 miles.
9. Barack Obama spent most of his childhood years in Honolulu.
10. It's the favorite vacation destination for the author of this book.

Anyone with Super Swagger who lives in Canada's winter climate visits Honolulu at least three times a year — or moves there for the entire winter!

Top 10 US Place Names with the Most Swagger

1. Noblesville, Indiana
2. Voltaire, North Dakota
3. Rambo Riviera, Arkansas
4. Uncle Sam, Louisiana
5. Frankenstein, Missouri
6. Hell, Michigan
7. Romance, Arkansas
8. Acres of Diamonds, Florida
9. Okay, Oklahoma
10. Gun Barrel City, Texas

A Swagger name for a town will make it sound exciting even if it is the most boring place in the country.

Top 10 US Street Names with the Most Swagger

1. Road to Happiness — Vermillion, Ohio
2. The Living End — Austin, Texas
3. None Such Place — New Castle, Delaware
4. Damn If I Know, Damn If I Care, Damn If I Will — Boca Grande, Florida
5. Ewe Turn — Kaysville, Utah
6. Almosta Road — Darby, Montana
7. Sir Galahad Drive — Riverside, California
8. This Ain't It Road —Dadeville, Alabama
9. Psycho Path — Traverse City, Michigan
10. Shades of Death Road — Great Meadows, New Jersey

A street name with Swagger is one that does not sound like a street name.

Top 10 Cities in Europe with the Most Swagger

1. Prague, Czechia
2. Paris, France
3. London, England
4. Istanbul, Turkey
5. Venice, Italy
6. Rome, Italy
7. Amsterdam, Netherlands
8. Barcelona, Spain
9. Vienna, Austria
10. Budapest, Hungary

The individual with Super Swagger will have visited both Prague and Istanbul, in addition to Paris and London — the four most remarkable European cities of them all.

Top 10 Reasons Why Prague Has Swagger

1. The Bistro Praha Restaurant in Edmonton is named after the city.
2. The movie "Amadeus" about Mozart was filmed in Prague.
3. The ninth century Prague Castle is recognized by the *Guinness Book of Records* as the largest castle complex in the world.
4. It's a mix of Baroque, Gothic, and Renaissance architecture.
5. The city's river Vltava has over 30 bridges and foot bridges.
6. Old Town Square has been its main marketplace for a millennium.
7. The astronomical clock in Old Town Square, installed in 1410, is the oldest operating clock of its kind on the planet.
8. Prague always has a lot of beer on hand because Czechs consume more beer per capita than any other country in the world.
9. The Charles Bridge is a masterpiece of 30 striking statues.
10. Czech cuisine, not a synonym for healthy eating, is fabulous.

Any European with Super Swagger — including Volodymyr Zelensky (in photo) — will have visited Prague.

Top 10 Reasons Why Paris Has Swagger

1. Paris is the most visited city in the world.
2. It is named after the Parisii, a Celtic people who settled on its central island — the Île de la Cité — in the 3rd century BC.
3. It's a fascinating city of pleasures particularly for the intelligent.
4. "As an artist, a man has no home in Europe save in Paris."
5. Ernest Hemingway was right saying, "Paris is a movable feast."
6. It's known as the "City of Lights" for its beauty and charm.
7. Because Parisians are keen filmgoers, there are over 100 theaters (théâtres) in Paris.
8. Authors Victor Hugo and Voltaire have a Paris Connection.
9. The Louvre houses the Mona Lisa (1503-1506) of Leonardo da Vinci and several ancient Greek statues such as Venus de Milo.
10. The Arc de Triomphe and the Madeleine are located here.

More American and British individuals with Swagger choose to go to Paris to die there than anywhere else.

Top 10 Reasons Why London Has Swagger

1. This vast metropolis is by far the largest city in Europe, a distinction it has maintained since the 17th century.
2. London is one of the world's major financial and cultural capitals.
3. The city's character is found in its diverse and distinct sections.
4. The historic Tower of London, a former prison, now holds the crown jewels of England.
5. The British Museum is one of the world's most famous museums.
6. The Tower Bridge, completed in 1894, is an icon of not only London, but also of the United Kingdom.
7. There are over 300 different languages spoken in London.
8. Unless a pathetic bore, you will never run out of things to do here.
9. For many great reasons, millions of foreigners want to live here.
10. The Chelsea soccer club has the most Swagger of any in Europe.

Having Swagger in London is ten times as powerful and rewarding as having Swagger anywhere in Russia.

Top 10 Reasons Why Istanbul Has Swagger

1. Its name is one of the most enchanting of city names representing its own code of food, architecture, literature, poetry, and music.
2. It's the only city in the world that sits astride two continents.
3. The Bosphorous separates its European and Asian sections.
4. Its many religious and historical sites are second to none.
5. Its Hagia Sophia was built between 532 and 537.
6. The Blue Mosque is one of the world's most famous mosques.
7. The city offers a deep dive into the rich Turkish culture.
8. The Grand Bazaar is one of the biggest and oldest covered shopping markets in the world offering practically everything.
9. The Spice Bazaar is a culinary and historic wonder.
10. At all its many fascinating markets, you are expected to bargain over the prices, which is a part of Turkish culture.

Individuals with Super Swagger will either try to conquer Istanbul or be prepared to have Istanbul conquer them.

Top 10 Reasons Why Venice Has Swagger

1. It's considered one of the most beautiful cities in the world.
2. The city is known as the "Queen of the Adriatic."
3. It's situated on 120 islands formed by 177 canals in a lagoon.
4. The islands are connected by 400 bridges.
5. The bridges in the old part of the city are for pedestrians only.
6. No motor vehicles are permitted on the narrow, winding lanes and streets that penetrate the old city.
7. This small city is one of the most visited cities in the world.
8. During the middle ages it was renowned worldwide for cultural and artistic development.
9. The Grand Canal divides it into two nearly equal portions.
10. The city's Adrian sea breeze will fan your face, feel native to your veins, and cool them into calmness!

Why wouldn't Venice have Swagger given that Truman Capote said,
"Venice is like eating an entire box of chocolate liqueurs at one go."

Top 10 Cities in Canada with the Most Swagger

1. Vancouver, British Columbia
2. Toronto, Ontario
3. Montréal, Quebec
4. Quebec City, Quebec
5. Victoria, British Columbia
6. Halifax, Nova Scotia
7. Calgary, Alberta
8. Winnipeg, Manitoba
9. Saskatoon, Saskatchewan
10. Kelowna, British Columbia

The Canadian individual with Super Swagger feels that Canada has only three cities: Vancouver, Toronto, and Montréal. Everywhere else in Canada is Fort McMurray.

Top 10 Reasons Why Vancouver Has Swagger

1. It's regularly listed as one of the most livable cities in the world.
2. It's one of the most expensive cities in the world to live in.
3. It's rated the luxury car capital of North America with many Ferraris, Lamborghinis, Rolls-Royces, and Bentleys on its streets.
4. It has one of the best winter climates in all of Canada.
5. The Pacific Ocean, the mighty forests, and the majestic mountains add to its spectacular surroundings.
6. It's a truly international city, a collage of cultures and wealth.
7. The Vancouver International Airport is regularly rated as the best airport in North America.
8. It's the home of billionaire Chip Wilson, the founder of Lululemon.
9. Its Stanley Park is one of the greatest urban parks in the world.
10. The author of this book calls Vancouver his second home.

The prosperous individual in Vancouver is one who can live there with great Financial Swagger making a living as a digital nomad.

Top 10 Reasons Why Toronto Has Swagger

1. The city is the largest metropolitan area in Canada by far.
2. It is recognized as the financial and cultural center of Canada.
3. Super rapper Drake calls the city home and actually lives here.
4. Foreign-born residents constitute over 42 percent of the population.
5. Toronto is second only to New York City for live theater in NA.
6. Toronto International Film Festival, held for two weeks every September, is one of the best-attended film festivals in the world.
7. Toronto Blue Jays won World Series in 1992 and 1993.
8. Toronto Raptors, a non-U.S. team, won the NBA championship.
9. Its International Airport is the largest airport in Canada.
10. Wherever else you are from in Canada, Toronto is a super big city.

The person with Swagger in Toronto subconsciously knows that the person with Swagger in Vancouver has quite a bit more Swagger.

Top 10 Reasons Why Montréal Has Swagger

1. Singer Leonard Cohen and writer Mordecai Richler lived here.
2. Montréal is the second-largest French-speaking city in the world.
3. More than half the population can speak both French and English.
4. In total, 80 languages are spoken in the Montréal region.
5. *Gourmet Magazine* dedicated an entire issue to Montréal.
6. Bars and restaurants serve alcohol from 11 a.m. to 3 a.m.
7. Montréal is the tango capital of North America.
8. Its Notre-Dame Basilica in Old Montréal is a Gothic masterpiece known far and wide and one of its great tourist attractions.
9. Its "underground city" has over 18 miles of pedestrian walkways.
10. Founded in 1642, it's one of the oldest cities in North America.

The individual with Super Swagger in Montréal speaks not only two languages but at least three or four.

Top 10 City Parks in the World with the Most Swagger

1. Stanley Park, Vancouver, B.C., Canada
2. Central Park, New York, NY, USA
3. Park Güell, Barcelona, Spain
4. Centennial Park, Sydney, Australia
5. Jardin du Luxembourg, Paris, France
6. Ibirapuera Park, São Paulo, Brazil
7. Golden Gate Park, San Francisco, CA, USA
8. Battersea Park, London, England
9. Ala Moana Park, Honolulu, HI, USA
10. William Hawrelak Park, Edmonton, AB, Canada

People with Swagger choose to run in a city park by themselves where no one else will bother them and where they can think creatively about how to make a big difference in this world.

The Top 10 Neighborhoods in the World with the Most Swagger

1. West End (Vancouver, B.C., Canada)
2. Colonia Americana (Guadalajara, Mexico)
3. Cais do Sodré (Lisbon, Portugal)
4. Wat Bo Village (Siem Reap, Cambodia)
5. Ridgewood (New York City, USA)
6. Mile End (Montreal, Canada)
7. Barrio Logan (San Diego, USA)
8. Shimokitazawa (Tokyo, Japan)
9. Cliftonville (Margate, UK)
10. Cours Julien (Marseille, France)

The individual with Elegant Swagger would rather live in a neighborhood filled with intelligent peasants than in one filled with blowhard pretentious rich people.

Top 10 Billionaires Ever with the Most Swagger

1. Elon Musk
2. Richard Branson
3. Chuck Feeney
4. Ted Turner
5. Oprah Winfrey
6. Michael Bloomberg
7. Elton John
8. Paul Allen
9. Chip Wilson
10. Roman Abramovich

"There's a certain part of the contented majority," stated renowned economist John Kenneth Galbraith, "who love anybody who is worth a billion dollars." Indeed, but a billionaire with Swagger is loved even more.

Top 10 Entrepreneurs Ever with the Most Swagger

1. Benjamin Franklin
2. Steve Jobs
3. Elon Musk
4. John D. Rockefeller
5. Andrew Carnegie
6. Thomas Edison
7. Henry Ford
8. Madam CJ Walker
9. Elizabeth Arden
10. Richard Branson

Successful Entrepreneurs with Swagger are truly creative and change the world for the better. The pathological critics, babbling bozos, and hounding haters who run down these entrepreneurs want to keep the world the way it is.

Top 10 Con Artists Ever with the Most Swagger

1. Charles Ponzi
2. Ivan Boesky
3. Michael Milken
4. Bernard Ebbers
5. Michael de Guzman
6. Raj Rajaratnam
7. Dennis Kozlowski
8. Michael Milken
9. Jeff Skilling
10. John Rigas

The con artist with Swagger feels that the legendary gambler "Canada Bill" Jones was right when he advised, "It is morally wrong to allow suckers to keep their money."

Top 10 Notorious Historical Figures
Ever with the Most Swagger

1. Attila the Hun
2. Ivan the Terrible
3. Catherine the Great
4. Billy the Kid
5. William the Conqueror
6. Julius Caesar
7. Richard the Lion-Hearted
8. Joan of Arc
9. Cleopatra
10. Zorba the Greek

Leaders with Super Swagger know that to lead greatly they must completely turn their backs on the idiots.

Top 10 World Leaders in the 20th Century with the Most Swagger

1. Winston Churchill
2. Theodore Roosevelt
3. Mohanddas K. Ghandi
4. Martin Luther King
5. Golda Meir
6. Nelson Mandela
7. Margaret Thatcher
8. Dwight D. Eisenhower
9. Woodrow Wilson
10. Charles de Gaulle

The duty of a leader with Swagger is to transform weakness into strength, problems into opportunities, obstacles into stepping stones, and disaster into superb accomplishment.

Top 10 World Leaders in the 21st Century with the Most Swagger

1. Volodymyr Zelensky President of Ukraine
2. Barack Obama, 44th President of the US
3. Boris Johnson, Prime Minister of the UK
4. Jacinda Ardern, Prime Minister of New Zealand
5. Benjamin Netanyahu, Prime Minister of Israel
6. Rodrigo Duterte, President of Philippines
7. Narendra Modi, Prime Minister of India
8. Shinzō Abe, Prime Minister of Japan
9. Jacques Chirac, President of France
10. Yulia Tymoshenko, Prime Minister of Ukraine

Leaders with Super Swagger listen to advice from the experts and then spectacularly ignore it as President Volodymyr Zelensky did proclaiming, "I don't need a ride. I need ammunition!"

Top 10 US Presidents Ever with the Most Swagger

1. Barack Obama
2. Ronald Reagan
3. Bill Clinton
4. Abraham Lincoln
5. George Washington
6. Thomas Jefferson
7. Franklin D. Roosevelt
8. Harry S. Truman
9. Woodrow Wilson
10. Jimmy Carter

Achievers with Elegant Swagger feel that when it comes to Swagger, ex-Presidents Barack Obama and Richard Nixon had nothing in common. Barack Obama was a Porsche and Richard Nixon was a wheel barrow.

Top 10 British Prime Ministers Ever with the Most Swagger

1. Winston Churchill
2. Margaret Thatcher
3. Boris Johnson
4. Tony Blair
5. Clement Attlee
6. Harold Macmillan
7. John Major
8. Arthur Wellesley, 1st Duke of Wellington
9. David Cameron
10. Benjamin Disraeli

The leader with Swagger will look destiny in the eye with great courage but will also realize that he or she is not God.

Top 10 Philosophers Ever with the Most Swagger

1. Aristotle
2. Plato
3. Socrates
4. Friedrich Nietzsche
5. Immanuel Kant
6. René Descartes
7. John Locke
8. David Hume
9. Thomas Aquinas
10. Confucius

A philosopher with Swagger is one who knows that without music, life would be a mistake.

Top 10 Spiritual Gurus Ever
with the Most Swagger

1. Jesus Christ
2. Buddha
3. Dali Lama
4. Lao Tzu
5. Indira Nehru Gandhi
6. Archbishop Desmond Tutu
7. Bhagwan Shree Rajneesh (Osho)
8. Maharishi Mahesh Yogi
9. Nelson Mandela
10. Werner Erhard

The guru Rajneesh once proclaimed, "Anyone can be a guru. You will always have fools following you." That's why achievers with Swagger avoid most modern-day gurus.

Top 10 Female Actors Ever with the Most Swagger

1. Sacheen Littlefeather
2. Elizabeth Taylor
3. Marilyn Monroe
4. Sophia Loren
5. Bo Derek
6. Cindy Crawford
7. Raquel Welch
8. Brigitte Bardot
9. Farrah Fawcett
10. Sharon Stone

Actors with Swagger do not try to push their way to the front ranks of their profession nor do they yearn for distinctions or rewards. They just act naturally and the rewards follow.

Top 10 Male Actors Ever with the Most Swagger

1. Clint Eastwood
2. Steve McQueen
3. Kirk Douglas
4. Al Pacino
5. Humphrey Bogart
6. John Wayne
7. Robert Di Niro
8. Tom Hanks
9. Tom Cruise
10. Harrison Ford

Swagger is not just saying great things about your self.
Humphrey Bogart showed Swagger by proclaiming, "I made more lousy pictures than any actor in history."

Top 10 US Radio Talk Show Hosts Ever with the Most Swagger

1. Howard Stern
2. Rush Limbaugh
3. Larry King
4. Don Imus
5. Dr. Laura Schlessinger
6. Paul Harvey
7. Art Bell
8. Barry Gray
9. Barry Farber
10. Sally Jessy Raphel

A radio talk show host with Super Swagger is one who you hate but one who you can't resist listening to.

Top 10 US TV Talk Show Hosts Ever
with the Most Swagger

1. David Letterman
2. Johnny Carson
3. Oprah Winfrey
4. Larry Saunders
5. Stephen Colbert
6. Conan O'Brien
7. Larry King
8. Jon Stewart
9. Jimmy Fallon
10. Merv Griffin

*Truth be known, people who live lives of quiet desperation
want to appear on a sensational TV talk show hosted by
an individual with Super Swagger.*

Top 10 US Celebrities with the Most Swagger Who Spent Time in Jail

1. Chuck Berry
2. James Brown
3. David Crosby
4. Billie Holiday
5. Sophia Loren
6. Robert Mitchum
7. Sean Penn
8. Mike Tyson
9. Mae West
10. Peter Rose

If you have only half as much Swagger as the late Chuck Berry had, you still have Super Swagger.

Top 10 Celebrity High-School Dropouts Ever with the Most Swagger

1. Cary Grant, actor
2. Billy Joel, singer/songwriter
3. John Major, British Prime Minister
4. Peter Jennings, ABC newscaster
5. Wayne Newton, singer
6. Tracey Ullman, actress
7. Lawrence Welk, bandleader
8. James Naismith, inventor of basketball
9. Ellen Burstyn, actress
10. George Carey, Archbishop of Canterbury

There's zero likelihood that your doctor, dentist, or university professor with Swagger is a high-school dropout. Your favorite actor, politician, or stockbroker with Swagger just might be.

Top 10 Celebrity Ex-Postal Workers Ever with the Most Swagger

1. Abraham Lincoln, US President
2. Rock Hudson, Actor
3. Conrad Hilton, Hotel Entrepreneur
4. Charles Lindbergh, Aviator
5. Dan Akroyd, Canadian Actor and Comedian
6. Bing Crosby, Singer and Actor
7. Walt Disney, Cartoonist and Film Producer
8. Charles Bukowski, Poet and Author
9. William Faulkner, Pulitzer Prize-Winning Novelist
10. Sherman Hemsley, Actor

The postal worker with Super Swagger no doubt will become an ex-postal worker in no time flat.

Top 10 Laziest Famous People Ever with the Most Swagger

1. Winston Churchill
2. Albert Einstein
3. W. Somerset Maugham
4. Charles Darwin
5. Picasso
6. Axl Rose (Guns and Roses)
7. Isaac Newton
8. Karl Marx
9. President Calvin Coolidge
10. Dmitri Mendeleev

The lazy character with Swagger feels that sophisticated idleness is a sure sign of nobility.

Top 10 Celebrities with the Most Swagger Who Were Diabetics

1. James Cagney
2. Miles Davis
3. Jack Benny
4. Larry King
5. Thomas Edison
6. Jerry Garcia
7. Ernest Hemingway
8. Jackie Robinson
9. Mahalia Jackson
10. Dr. Phil McGraw

Many people diagnosed with diabetes think they are going to die early. Individuals with Super Swagger diagnosed with diabetes are immediately bound and determined to outlive all the people who don't have diabetes.

Top 10 Famous Night Owls with the Most Swagger

1. Barack Obama
2. Winston Churchill
3. Prince
4. Fran Lebowitz
5. J.R.R. Tolkien
6. John Travolta
7. Bob Dylan
8. Carl Jung
9. Christina Aguilera
10. Fidel Castro

The night owl with Elegant Swagger knows studies show that night owls are as healthy and wise as morning types — and a little bit wealthier. Night owls are also more open to new experiences and seek them out more.

Top 10 Signatures of Famous People with the Most Swagger Ever

1. Pablo Picasso
2. Marilyn Monroe
3. Michael Jackson
4. Diego Maradona
5. Walt Disney
6. Bruce Lee
7. John Hancock
8. Babe Ruth
9. Victoria Beckman
10. Clint Eastwood

Individuals with Swagger don't waste their time collecting other people's autographs. They spend their time constructively making their own autograph worth collecting.

Top 10 Birds in the World with the Most Swagger

1. Homeless Rooster in Honolulu
2. Southern Cassowary
3. European Herring Gull
4. Mute Swan
5. Great Northern Loon
6. Lammergeier (Bearded Vulture)
7. Red-tailed Hawk
8. Great Horned Owl
9. Whooping Crane
10. Ostrich

The rooster has Super Swagger because it takes full credit for the sun rising every morning.

Top 10 Animals in the World
with the Most Swagger

1. Homeless Rooster in Honolulu
2. Whale
3. Elephant
4. Hippopotamus
5. Gorilla
6. Rhinoceros
7. Dolphin
8. Giraffe
9. Bear
10. Jaguar

The rooster has the most Swagger because it's so small and thinks it can easily beat up any other animal in the world.

Top 10 Airline International First and Business Class Flights with the Most Swagger

1. Singapore Airlines
2. Emirates
3. Qatar Airways
4. Cathay Pacific
5. Turkish Airlines
6. Etihad
7. Asiana
8. Japan Airlines
9. All Nippon Airways
10. Air New Zealand

Achievers with Super Swagger don't fly overseas unless they can fly International Business Class or First Class.

Top 10 Airline International Flights in Premium Economy with the Most Swagger

1. Emirates
2. Qantas
3. All Nippon Airways
4. Virgin Atlantic
5. Singapore Airlines
6. Scandinavian Airlines
7. Cathay Pacific
8. Latam Airlines
9. Air Canada
10. American Airlines

Achievers with Super Swagger let their dreams take flight whether they are on an airplane or on the ground.

Top 10 Airline Amenities with the Most Swagger

1. First class shower suite on Emirates A380
2. Double bed in suite on Singapore Airlines A380
3. Three Room Suite with a Butler on Eithad A380
4. Business class bar on Qatar Airways A380
5. Business class lounge on Korean Air A380
6. Virtual windows on Emirates 777 First Class
7. Video room service on Emirates 777 first class
8. 32-Inch Touch screen on Singapore Airlines A380
9. Pre-Select Dining on Qatar Airways First Class
10. In-Flight Chef on Eithad A380

Individuals with Super Swagger like to have a shower when flying International Business Class. They also like to have a shower in the Arrivals Lounge at their destination.

Top 10 North American Airlines
with the Most Swagger

1. Air Canada
2. United Airlines
3. Alaska Airlines
4. Hawaiian Airlines
5. Delta
6. Southwest Airlines
7. JetBlue Airlines
8. Frontier Airlines
9. American
10. Westjet

Many people with Swagger fly Business Class and International Business Class because they know that they may end up meeting someone important with Swagger.

Top 10 Airlines with the Most Swagger
That Went Totally Broke in the 1980s

1. The Lord's Airline (for born-again believers flying to Tel Aviv)
2. The Great American Smoker's Club (Airline just for smokers)
3. Pride Air (shut down after only three months in business)
4. Presidential Airways (full-service airline at discount prices)
5. Highland Express (offered a $25 ticket from Scotland to Newark)
6. Challenge International Airlines (name didn't inspire confidence)
7. The Hawaii Express (jammed Boeing 747s with 501 seats)
8. People Express (customers paid for their tickets onboard)
9. Trump Shuttle (Trump bailed out after losing $125 million.)
10. MGM Grand Air (all-first-class airline with no economy seats)

The character with Raunchy Swagger is not afraid of flying.
In fact, he is afraid of not flying.

Top 10 Passenger Airplanes Ever
with the Most Swagger

1. Concorde
2. Boeing 747
3. Airbus A380
4. Airbus A350
5. Gulfstream G-650
6. Airbus A320
7. Embracer E175
8. Lockheed Electra
9. L1011
10. Douglas DC-3

Individuals with Swagger flew from London to New York on a Concorde not to save three hours — but because they loved flying on a miracle.

Top 10 International Airports in the World with the Most Swagger

1. Singapore Changi
2. Doha Hamad
3. Tokyo Haneda
4. Tokyo Narita
5. Seoul Incheon
6. Paris CDG
7. Munich
8. Istanbul
9. Zurich
10. Kansai

Achievers with Super Swagger flying internationally have at least two airline premium lounges to choose from where they can relax and contemplate their next creative ventures.

Top 10 International Airports in North America with the Most Swagger

1. Vancouver
2. Seattle-Tacoma
3. Houston George Bush
4. Cincinnati/Northern Kentucky
5. Denver
6. Atlanta
7. Toronto Pearson
8. Dallas/Fort Worth
9. San Francisco
10. Montréal

The achiever with Swagger flying out of the Vancouver International Airport is usually flying Business Class to somewhere exotic such as Tokyo, Hong Kong, or Bangkok.

Top 10 Airport Lounges in the World with the Most Swagger

1. Emirates First Class Lounge, Dubai
2. Air France La Première Lounge, Paris
3. Cathay Pacific The Pier First Class Lounge, Hong Kong
4. Delta Sky Club, Atlanta
5. Lufthansa First Class Terminal, Frankfurt
6. Qantas First Lounge, Sydney
7. Qatar Airways Al Mourjan Business Lounge, Doha
8. Swiss First Class Lounge, Zurich
9. United Polaris Lounge, Chicago
10. Virgin Atlantic Clubhouse, London

Minimally, an airport lounge with Swagger has shower facilities for its patrons in addition to delicious food and superb wine.

Top 10 Luxury Train Rides in the World with the Most Swagger

1. Rocky Mountaineer, Canada
2. Venice Simplon-Orient-Express, Italy
3. The Blue Train, South Africa
4. Belmond British Pullman, United Kingdom
5. Eastern and Oriental Express, Singapore/Malaysia/Thailand
6. Bernina Express, Switzerland/Italy
7. Coast Starlight, USA
8. Belmond Royal Scotsman, Scotland
9. The Ghan, Australia
10. California Zephyr, USA

There is no luxury train the character with Raunchy Swagger wouldn't take, regardless where it's going.

Top 10 Movies Ever with the Most Swagger

1. The Godfather
2. Star Wars
3. Jaws
4. The Exorcist
5. The Sting
6. Gone With the Wind
7. Casablanca
8. Bullitt
9. The Good, the Bad, and the Ugly
10. American Graffiti

*One of the joys of going to the movies for the person with
Raunchy Swagger is to see how trashy movies can be.*

Top 10 Movies Ever with the Least Swagger

1. Attack of the Killer Tomatoes
2. Cars That Eat People
3. A Thousand Words
4. Gotti
5. Pinocchio
6. Superbabies: Baby Geniuses 2
7. Gold Diggers
8. Jaws the Revenge
9. The Ridiculous 6
10. Return to the Blue Lagoon

Individuals with Raunchy Swagger won't ever get tired of trashy movies but at the same time they won't ever be inspired to greater heights watching them.

Top 10 Movie Cars Ever with the Most Swagger

1. James Bond's 1964 Aston Martin DB5 in *Goldfinger*
2. Steve McQueen's GT390 Fastback Mustang in *Bullitt*
3. 1941 Packard Custom Super One-Eighty in *The Godfather*
4. 1976 Lotus Esprit Series in *The Spy Who Loved Me*
5. 1970 Dodge Charger in *The Fast & Furious*
6. 1968 Aston Mk I Mini Cooper S in *The Italian Job*
7. 1959 Cadillac Miller-Meteor Ambulance in *Ghostbusters*
8. 1980 Lamborghini Countach LP 400S in *The Cannonball Run*
9. 1932 Customized Ford Deuce Coupe in *American Graffiti*
10. 1977 Pontiac Trans Am in *Smokey and the Bandit*

*The achiever with Super Swagger will not lend his $350,000
Aston Martin Vanquish to anyone whom he has sired.*

Top 10 Movie Cars Ever with the Least Swagger

1. 1973 XB GT Ford Falcon, *Mad Max*
2. 1959 Cadillac Miller-Meteor Ectomobile, *Ghostbusters 1*
3. 1974 Dodge Monaco – Bluesmobile, *The Blues Brothers*
4. 1958 Plymouth Fury, *Christine*
5. 1992 Ford Explorer XLT UN46, *Jurassic Park*
6. 1976 AMC Pacer, Mirthmobile, *Wayne's World 1 and 2*
7. 1973 Ford Gran Torino, *The Big Lebowski*
8. 1979 Ford LTD Country Squire, *National Lampoon's Vacation*
9. 1984 Ford Econoline, *Dumb and Dumber*
10. 1997 Chevrolet 2500 Silverado Fleetside, *Kill Bill: Vol. 1*

The achiever with Super Swagger knows how to drive a
stick-shift standard automobile. Indeed, he prefers it over
any automatic even if the automatic is a Tesla.

Top 10 Super Cars Ever with the Most Swagger

1. Lamborghini Aventador
2. Audi R8
3. Lamborghini Huracan
4. Ferrari 458
5. Lamborghini Gallardo
6. McLaren P1
7. Honda/Acura NSX
8. Ferrari LaFerrari
9. Bugatti Veyron
10. Bugatti Chiron

Characters with Swagger may enjoy driving a Lamborghini Aventador but don't be surprised to see them joyfully driving a raunchy, rusted-out 1995 Camry 2-door coupe.

Top 10 German Classic Cars Ever
with the Most Swagger

1. Porsche 356 Speedster
2. Porsche 911
3. BMW 328 Roadster
4. 1955 Mercedes-Benz 300 SL Gullwing
5. BMW 507
6. Porsche 550 Spyder
7. BMW M1
8. RUF CTR 'Yellowbird'
9. Audi Quattro
10. Mercedes-Benz 190 SL

There are many rational arguments for not buying a Porsche — but achievers with Super Swagger don't want to be bored by them.

Top 10 Sports Car Ever with the Most Swagger

1. Porsche 911 Turbo S
2. Chevrolet Corvette
3. Lamborghini Countach
4. Ferrari Daytona
5. Mercedes Benz 300L Coupe
6. Dodge Viper
7. Nissan Z-Car
8. Toyota Supra Mark IV
9. Acura NSX
10. Shelby 289 Cobra

A Porsche 911 Turbo S has Super Swagger because it looks like a Porsche 911 Turbo S — and nothing else!

Top 10 Cars Ever with the Least Swagger

1. AMC Gremlin
2. Ford Pinto
3. Trabant
4. Yugo
5. Lada
6. Fiat Multipla
7. Aston Martin Lagonda
8. Nissan Cube
9. Pontiac Aztek
10. Volkswagen Type 181

The guy with Raunchy Swagger can drive an AMC Gremlin and actually make other people envious of him. His adage is, "Real men drive the car they damn well want to drive."

Top 10 SUVs with the Most Swagger

1. Porsche Cayenne Turbo GT
2. Mercedes Benz G Class
3. Bentley Bentayga
4. Rolls Royce
5. Maserati Grecale
6. Lamborghini Urus
7. Austin Martin DBX
8. BMW X5 M
9. Ferrari Purosangue
10. Alfa Romeo Stelvio

The only SUV with as much Swagger as a Porsche Cayenne Turbo GT is another Porsche Cayenne Turbo GT exactly like it except for the color.

Top 10 American Classic Cars from the 1950s and 1960s with the Most Swagger

1. 1963 Chevy Corvette Stingray
2. 1964 Ford Mustang
3. 1957 Chev 2-dr hardtop (or convertible)
4. 1964 Chevrolet Impala SS 2-dr hardtop
5. 1957 Ford Hardtop Convertible
6. 1967 Chev Camaro
7. 1966 Chevelle 2 door hardtop
8. 1957 Ford Thunderbird
9. 1957 Chevrolet Corvette C1
10. 1965 Plymouth Barracuda

A snappy car is important to people with Super Swagger.
They get migraine headaches when they drive a Volvo.

The Top 10 American Classic Cars of All Time with the Most Swagger

1. Ford Model T (1908)
2. Duesenberg J (1935)
3. Chrysler Airflow (1934)
4. Tucker Torpedo (1948)
5. Chevrolet Corvette Sting Ray (1963)
6. Shelby AC Cobra (1962)
7. Chevrolet Tri Five (1955 to 1957)
8. Cadillac Eldorado (1953)
9. Ford Mustang (1964)
10. Ford Thunderbird (1955)

When buying a used car, the chap with Elegant Swagger checks the stations on the car radio. If they are all on rock and roll, he knows that the transmission is shot.

The Top 10 American Muscle Cars Ever with the Most Swagger

1. 1964 Pontiac GTO Tri-Power
2. 1965 Shelby Mustang GT-350
3. 1970 Chevrolet Chevelle SS 454
4. 1967 Chevrolet Camaro Z/28
5. 1971 Plymouth Hemi Barracuda
6. 1968 Chevrolet Corvette L88
7. 1970 Ford Mustang Boss 302
8. 1969 Pontiac Firebird 400 Coupe
9. 1970 Plymouth Road Runner Superbird
10. 1971 Buick GSX with Stage-1 Performance Pack

The GTO had so much Swagger that the single of the song "Little GTO" written about it by Ronnie and the Daytonas sold over 1,000,000 copies and was awarded a gold disc.

Top 10 Foods in the World with the Most Swagger

1. White Pearl Albino Caviar
2. Swallow's Nest Soup
3. White Truffles
4. Dry Cured Jamón Ibérico Ham
5. Japanese Wagyu Steaks
6. Kopi Luwak Coffee
7. Matsutake Mushrooms
8. Moose Cheese
9. Angio Hair Sergio made with Ayam Cemani Black Chicken
10. Fugu Fish

One must be careful with Swaggerific foods. If a certain type of food tastes super good, it's likely trying to kill you.

Top 10 Foods in the World with the Least Swagger

1. SPAM
2. Candy Corn
3. Bologna
4. Eggplant Parmesan
5. Sweet Potato Pie
6. Brussel Sprouts
7. Liver
8. Lemon Meringue Pie
9. Pop Tarts
10. Chicken Pot Pie

The guy with Raunchy Swagger knows that there are 12.8 cans of SPAM products eaten every second but he still refuses to eat SPAM regardless of how it's prepared.

Top 10 Ethnic Foods with the Most Swagger

1. Italian
2. French
3. East Indian
4. Spanish
5. Chinese
6. Greek
7. Lebanese
8. Japanese
9. Thai
10. Mexican

Italian food without any doubt has the most Swagger.
The problem with Italian food, however, is that after two
or three days you are hungry again.

Top 10 Ethnic Foods with the Least Swagger

1. Finish
2. Peruvian
3. Filipino
4. Cuban
5. Dutch
6. Brazilian
7. British
8. Russian
9. Belgium
10. American

The reason that the British became determined explorers with Swagger is they were in search of a decent meal.

Top 10 Italian Swagger Dishes in the World Worth Traveling For

1. Angel Hair Sergio (Edmonton)
2. Pizza Napoletana (Naples)
3. Lasagna (Bologna)
4. Ossobuco alla Milanese (Milan)
5. Panzanella (Tuscany)
6. Focaccia (Liguria)
7. Spaghetti alla Carbonara (Rome)
8. Cicchetti (Venice)
9. Caponata (Sicily)
10. Burrata (Puglia)

No doubt Italian dishes have the most Swagger. Results don't lie. Italy happens to be a poor country full of rich people because of the sensational food they eat.

Top 10 Restaurants in the World with the Most Swagger

1. Sublimotion, Ibiza, Spain
2. Masa, New York, US
3. Maison Pic Valence, Paris, France
4. Restaurant De L'Hôtel De Ville, Crissier, Switzerland
5. Kitcho Arashiyama, Tokyo, Japan
6. Guy Savoy, Paris, France
7. Per Se, New York, US
8. Ultraviolet, Shanghai, China
9. Aragawa, Tokyo, Japan
10. Ithaa Undersea, Rangali Island, Maldives

People with Elegant Swagger eat with their intelligence and not with their stomach. They never leave even the finest of restaurants with the inward feeling of being a pig.

Top 10 Restaurants in New York Ever
with the Most Swagger

1. Masa
2. The Chef's Table at Brooklyn Fare
3. Jean-Georges
4. Le Bernardin
5. Momofuku Ko
6. Per Se
7. Daniel
8. Eleven Madison Park
9. Bâtard
10. Ugly Baby

Achievers with Elegant Swagger eat to live and don't
live to eat. As the wise Benjamin Franklin pointed out,
"Three good meals a day is bad living."

Top 10 Restaurants in London Ever with the Most Swagger

1. The Ivy
2. The Swan, Shakespeare's Globe
3. Sexy Fish
4. Chiltern Firehouse
5. Restaurant Ours
6. Hakkasan Mayfair
7. Nobu
8. Pied à Terre
9. Berner's Tavern
10. Made in Italy

To the character with Raunchy Swagger vegetables may elicit some interest but lack much meaning if not accompanied by a delicious cut of meat.

Top 10 Restaurants in Toronto Ever with the Most Swagger

1. Casa Don Alfonso 1890
2. Canoe Restaurant and Bar
3. The Keg Mansion
4. Hard Rock Café
5. Fred's Not Here
6. Scaramouche Restaurant
7. Alo Restaurant
8. 7 West
9. Trattoria Primavera Ristorante
10. Barberian's Steak House

Individuals with Elegant Swagger can usually get a table in a full high-end restaurant because of the money they spend there, the tips they give, and the charm they bring.

Top 10 Restaurants in Vancouver, B.C. Ever with the Most Swagger

1. Francesco's Ristorante Italia
2. Joe Fortes
3. Hy's Mansion Steakhouse
4. Umberto's
5. Tavola
6. Vij's
7. Naam
8. Raincity Grill
9. Stormin Norman's Spirit Grill
10. Bishops

The character with Raunchy Swagger always carries a bottle of Tabasco sauce to a fine restaurant just in case.

Top 10 Restaurants in Edmonton Ever with the Most Swagger

1. Rigoletto's Café
2. Bistro Praha
3. Cosmos
4. Waldens
5. The Steak Loft
6. Café Select
7. Carvery
8. Table de la Renoir
9. The Stage Door
10. La Petit Iza

Just because a restaurant is more than 200 feet above the ground and revolves around once every hour doesn't mean that it has any Swagger.

Top 10 Restaurant Names in the World Ever with the Most Swagger

1. Fred's Not Here — Toronto, ON
2. Killer Pizza from Mars — Oceanside, CA
3. Leaping Lizard Café — Virginia Beach, VA
4. The Notorious P.I.G. — Missoula, Montana
5. Tequila Mockingbird — Ocean City, Maryland
6. The Angry Avocado — The Dalles, OR
7. The Holy Grail Pub — Plano, TX
8. Codfather — Reno, NV
9. Thai Tanic — Washington, D.C.
10. Curry in a Hurry — New York, NY

At a restaurant with a large table and many seats, the seat that the achiever with Super Swagger sits in is undoubtedly always the head of the table.

Top 10 New Restaurant Names
with the Most Swagger

1. Incredibly Italian
2. Hotter Than Hell Curry House
3. Donald Just Left
4. Too Sophisticated for Oprah
5. Darwin's Diner — No Dummies Allowed!
6. Proof Is in the Wine
7. First We Take Manhattan
8. Midnight Buzz
9. Cleopatra's Castle Café
10. Attila the Hun's Holier than Thou Bar-b-Q Grill

The favorite lunch of the character with Raunchy Swagger is a gourmet hot dog with vintage wine. This beats anything with capers and fizzled water.

Top 10 New Restaurant Names
with the Least Swagger

1. Probably Pizza
2. Die Today Diner
3. Uncontrollably British Cuisine
4. Pedestrian Pretzels
5. Angela Did Not Die Here
6. Trollers' Treats
7. The Devil May Be Here Soon
8. Credibly Caucasian
9. Russian Roulette
10. La Petit Bourgeois

The name of a restaurant is irrelevant to the person with
Swagger if the wine is a farce and the food a tragedy.

Top 10 Bars in the World with the Most Swagger

1. The Connaught Bar, London
2. Paradiso, Barcelona
3. Tayēr + Elementary, London
4. Little Red Door, Paris
5. Two Schmucks, Barcelona
6. Katana Kitten, New York
7. Jigger & Pony, Singapore
8. Florería Atlántico, Buenos Aires
9. Licorería Limantour, Mexico City
10. Satan's Whiskers, London

*Individuals with Elegant Swagger occasionally go into a bar
for a drink or two — but they do not make it a hobby.*

Top 10 Coffee Bars in the World
with the Most Swagger

1. Le Consulat Café, Montmartre, Paris, France
2. Starbucks, Pike Market, Seattle, WA, USA
3. Jonas Reindl, Vienna, Austria
4. Ditta Artigianale, Florence, Italy
5. Barristart Coffee, Singapore
6. El Café, Havanna, Cuba
7. Café SAT, Montreal, Canada
8. La Fontaine de Belleville, Paris, France
9. Café Tortoni, Buenos Aires, Argentina
10. Island Vintage Coffee, Honolulu, Hawaii, USA

Characters with Raunchy Swagger like to drink their coffee
in accordance with the Turkish preference: "Black as hell,
strong as death, sweet as love."

Top 10 Canadian Coffee Bars
with the Most Swagger

1. Sugarbowl, Edmonton, AB
2. Caffè Italia, Montreal, PQ
3. The Ministry of Coffee and Social Affairs, Ottawa, ON
4. Maderas Café, Toronto, ON
5. Revolver, Vancouver, BC
6. The Roasterie, Calgary, AB
7. Barocco x Nino, Toronto, ON
8. Espresso 46, Halifax, NS
9. The Battery Café, St. John's, NL
10. Broadway Roastery, Saskatoon, SK

Achievers with Elegant Swagger who have visited the Sugarbowl include Connor McDavid of the Edmonton Oilers. They also include cool dudes in snappy MGBs.

Top 10 Types of Coffee with the Most Swagger

1. Cowboy Coffee
2. Kopi Luwak coffee
3. Killer Coffee
4. Espresso
5. Cappuccino
6. Americano
7. Ristretto
8. Death Wish
9. Red Eye
10. Kona Peaberry

Elegant Swagger is drinking Americano at Starbucks.
Super Swagger is drinking Killer Coffee in Australia.
Raunchy Swagger is drinking Cowboy Coffee wherever you are.

Top 10 Liqueurs in the World with the Most Swagger

1. Jägermeister
2. Grand Marnier
3. Capairi
4. Baileys Irish Cream
5. Amaretto
6. Cointreau
7. Frangelico
8. Kahlúa
9. St-Germain
10. Sambuca

The Raunchy Swagger person's first impression of Jägermeister: "Like Cannibalism — a matter of taste."

The Top 10 Liquors in the World with the Most Swagger

1. Bruichladdich X4 Quadrupled Whiskey — Scotland
2. Spirytus Vodka — Poland
3. Everclear Grain Alcohol — US
4. River Antoine Royale Grenadian Rum — Grenada
5. Hapsburg Gold Label Premium Reserve Absinthe — Czechia
6. Pincer Shanghai Strength Vodka — Scotland
7. Balkan 176 Vodka — Bulgaria
8. John Crow Batty Rum — Jamaica
9. Bacardi 151 — Puerto Rico
10. King of Spirits Absinthe — Czechia

The person with Raunchy Swagger prefers Bruichladdich X4 Quadrupled Whiskey because BBC journalists proved that it can power a sports car at speeds over 100 mph.

Top 10 Alcoholic Drinks with the Most Swagger

1. Martini
2. Belline
3. Margarita
4. Moscow Mule
5. Mojito
6. Whiskey Sour
7. Manhattan
8. Champagne
9. Bourborn
10. Ceasar

In regards to martinis, the person with Raunchy Swagger is like Homer Simpson who once quipped, "My bartender knows just how I like my martini – full of alcohol."

Top 10 Vintage Wines with the Most Swagger

1. 1992 Screaming Eagle Cabernet Sauvignon, USA
2. 2013 Leroy Domaine d'Auvenay Chevalier-Montrachet Grand Cru, Cote de Beaune, France
3. 1976 Egon Muller Scharzhofberger Riesling, Germany
4. 1869 Chateau Lafite Rothschild, Pauillac, France
5. 1978 Giacomo Conterno Monfortino, Barolo Riserva, Italy
6. 1990 Dom Pérignon P3 Plenitude Brut, Champagne, France
7. 2008 Teso La Monja, Toro, Spain
8. 2014 Descendientes de J. Palacios La Faraona, Bierzo, Spain
9. Blandy's MCDXIX The Winemaker's Selection, Portugal
10. 2001 Catena Zapata Estiba Reservada, Agrelo, Argentina

At a wine tasting the individual with Elegant Swagger will declare either, "The bouquet is better than the taste," or "The taste is better than the bouquet."

Top 10 Medium Priced Wines in the World with the Most Swagger

1. The Mollydooker Shiraz hat trick, Australia
2. Grgich Hills 2016 Chardonnay, Napa Valley, USA
3. 2005 Bodegas Roda Cirsion, Spain
4. 2007 Concha y Toro Carmín de Peumo Carmenère, Chile
5. 2007 Nosotros, Argentina
6. 2008 Spottswoode Cabernet Sauvignon, California
7. 2007 Gaja Barbaresco, Italy
8. 2007 Sassicaia, Italy
9. 2009 Tridente, Spain
10. 2018 Oculus, Mission Hill Family Estate, Canada

The character with Raunchy Swagger never tastes fine wine first. He just instructs the Sommelier to fill up the glasses and not waste any precious time for anyone.

Top 10 Bum Wines Ever with the Most Swagger

1. Thunderbird
2. Night Train Express
3. Wild Irish Rose
4. Cisco Strawberry
5. MD 20/20 Blue Raspberry
6. Ripple
7. Broke Ass Red Blend
8. Bright's Pale Dry Select Sherry
9. Boones Farm
10. Buckfast Tonic Wine

Adventurous individuals with Swagger occasionally have a Bum Wine Party when they feature $1.99 bottles of street wine along with Mondelēz spray cheese.

Top 10 Beer Brands in the World with the Most Swagger

1. Tuborg Classic
2. Czech Hbor
3. Budweiser
4. Miller High Life
5. Stella
6. Carlsburg
7. Erdinger
8. Coors
9. Hawker Munich Gold
10. Kokane

The character with Raunchy Swagger feels that when the water in a place is suspect, it's best to drink an alternative liquid that has been filtered through a tub of malt.

Top 10 Fruits with the Most Swagger

1. Apple
2. Lemon
3. Jackfruit
4. Durian
5. Rambutan
6. Mangosteen
7. Jabuticaba
8. Australian Finger Lime
9. Hala Fruit
10. Miracle Berry

The apple has the most Swagger, because as Henry David Thoreau proclaimed, "The apple is the noblest of fruits."

Top Ten Apples Ever with the Most Swagger

1. The one that Eve ate
2. The one that Steve Jobs built
3. The one that bounced off Isaac Newton's head
4. The Big Apple (New York)
5. The Apple of Mortality, Snow White and the Seven Dwarves
6. The Apple of Accuracy, William Tell
7. The Apple of Discord, Greek mythology
8. The Apple of Trickery, Atalanta
9. The Apple of Immortality, Norse mythology
10. The Divine Apple – Avalon

To the individual with Elegant Swagger, Newton's apple and Steve Job's apple are more connected than first meets the human eye.

10 Top 10 Activities with the Most Swagger

1. Drinking a bottle of 1982 Chateau Latour with Julio Iglesias while flying International Business Class on a Dreamliner
2. Being a guest musician in a famous rock group
3. Taking the Rocky Mountaineer train trip in Canada
4. White-water rafting the Ayung River in Bali
5. Climbing Mount Kilimanjaro, the highest mountain in Africa
6. Scuba dive among sunken ships in the Caribbean
7. Writing a book for a $1,000,000 advance
8. Flying to the Swiss Alps for a massage at an exclusive spa
9. Experiencing dog sledding in Alaska
10. Heli-skiing the Canadian Rockies

The character with Super Swagger drinks hedonistic wines
such as 1982 Chateau Latour even when alone.

Top 10 Activities with the Least Swagger

1. Standing in line for anything
2. Doing laundry
3. Commuting to work
4. Weeding the garden
5. Opening junk mail
6. Attending corporate meetings
7. Cleaning the house
8. Writing an autobiography when you are a total bore
9. Saving/using coupons and looking for senior discounts
10. Taking part in any socialist protest march

Individuals with Swagger never wait in line at a hipster breakfast restaurant. One of the reasons is that they dislike waiting in line almost as much as they dislike hipsters.

Top 10 Sports in the World with the Most Swagger

1. Hockey
2. Basketball
3. Soccer
4. Tennis
5. NFL Football
6. Baseball
7. Boxing
8. Bicycle Racing at the Tour de France
9. Downhill Skiing
10. Car Racing

Hockey has the most Swagger because of its ferocity and skill — and because Mark Messier played the game.

Top 10 Sports in the World with the Least Swagger

1. Golf
2. Curling
3. Pickleball
4. Bowling
5. Poker
6. Rugby
7. Cricket
8. Cross Country Skiing
9. Badminton
10. Squash

Golf has the least Swagger because it's so slow and nothing much ever happens. Moreover, it does little for one's physical conditioning compared to hockey and basketball.

Top 10 Male Tennis Players Ever with the Most Swagger

1. John McEnroe
2. Jimmy Connors
3. Bjorn Borg
4. Ivan Lendl
5. Andre Agassi
6. Arthur Ashe
7. Ilie Năstase
8. Rafael Nadal
9. Pete Sampras
10. Boris Becker

The tennis player with Raunchy Swagger will put as much forward spin on the tennis ball as he or she can in a valiant attempt to fleece the cover off the ball.

Top 10 Female Tennis Players Ever with the Most Swagger

1. Maria Sharapova
2. Serena Williams
3. Billie Jean King
4. Martina Navratilova
5. Chris Evert
6. Martina Hingis
7. Steffi Graf
8. Venus Williams
9. Monica Seles
10. Caroline Wozniacki

If tennis players with Swagger such as Maria Sharapova know that they're going to lose, they do it with class.

Top 10 Soccer Players Ever with the Most Swagger

1. Thierry Henry
2. George Best
3. Diego Maradona
4. Pelé
5. Francesco Totti
6. Eric Cantona
7. Ronaldo
8. Messi
9. Zinedine Zidane
10. Cristiano Ronaldo

Soccer players with Swagger such as Thierry Henry never play for the tie. They go full out for the win.

Top 10 NBA Players Ever with the Most Swagger

1. Dennis Rodman
2. Michael Jordon
3. Magic Johnson
4. Larry Bird
5. LeBron James
6. Kobe Bryant
7. Steve Nash
8. Pistol Pete Maravich
9. Jamal Crawford
10. Allen Iverson

More than any other sport, professional basketball has its share of characters with Swagger. Indeed, Swagger runs rampant throughout the hardwood.

Top 10 Baseball Players Ever with the Most Swagger

1. Reggie Jackson
2. Babe Ruth
3. Willie Mays
4. Johnny Bench
5. Derek Jeter
6. Frank Robinson
7. Mickey Mantle
8. Ricky Henderson
9. Roger Clemens
10. Jose Batista

A major league baseball player with Super Swagger can be a guy being disgustingly cocky and repulsive or remarkably amusing and easy to embrace.

Top 10 NHL Players Ever with the Most Swagger

1. Mark Messier
2. Bret Hull
3. Gordie Howe
4. Rocket Richard
5. Bobby Orr
6. Eddie Shack
7. Lanny MacDonald
8. Guy Lafleur
9. Bobby Hull
10. Derek Sanderson

Not every professional hockey player boasts an abundance of Swagger, but those who do are the ones we will remember most fondly.

Top 10 Professional Wrestlers Ever
with the Most Swagger

1. Hulk Hogan
2. The Undertaker (Mark William Calaway)
3. Randy Savage
4. Shawn Michaels
5. James Hellwig
6. André the Giant
7. Roddy Piper
8. Ric Flair
9. Bret Hart
10. Junkyard Dog

Professional wrestlers with Swagger don't necessarily know what they are talking about. Keep in mind that "to wrestle" means to strive in an effort to master something.

Top 10 Soccer Teams Ever with the Most Swagger

1. Chelsea
2. Liverpool
3. Bayern Munich
4. Barcelona
5. Manchester United
6. Real Madrid
7. AC Milan
8. Arsenal
9. Inter Milan
10. Dynamo Kiev

You won't find many Americans with Swagger at a Chelsea soccer match but you will find a lot of fans from opposing teams who falsely think they have Swagger.

Top 10 NBA Teams Ever with the Most Swagger

1. Boston Celtics
2. Chicago Bulls
3. Los Angeles Lakers
4. Miami Heat
5. Detroit Pistons
6. Philadelphia 76ers
7. Golden State Warriors
8. San Antonio Spurs
9. Houston Rockets
10. New York Knicks

Just because a star basketball player can dunk a ball with Swagger doesn't mean that the individual is a great role model for your kids.

Top 10 NFL Teams Ever with the Most Swagger

1. New England Patriots
2. Pittsburg Steelers
3. San Francisco 49ers
4. Dallas Cowboys
5. Denver Broncos
6. Green Bay Packers
7. New Orleans Saints
8. Indianapolis Colts
9. Minnesota Vikings
10. New York Giants

If you think that NFL football is a stupid sport without much Swagger, then please tell us something worth listening to about golf.

Top 10 Major League Baseball Teams Ever with the Most Swagger

1. New York Yankees
2. Boston Red Sox
3. Cincinnati Reds
4. Pittsburgh Pirates
5. Baltimore Orioles
6. Detroit Tigers
7. Chicago Cubs
8. New York Mets
9. Atlanta Braves
10. Toronto Blue Jays

Baseball has Swagger if for no other reason than that it enables a player to fashion his personal freedom and financial independence to a level that most only dream of.

Top 10 National Hockey League Teams Ever with the Most Swagger

1. Edmonton Oilers
2. Montreal Canadians
3. Philadelphia Flyers
4. Detroit Red Wings
5. Toronto Maple Leafs
6. New York Rangers
7. Boston Bruins
8. New York Islanders
9. Chicago Black Hawks
10. Calgary Flames

To the hockey player with Raunchy Swagger every "boo" on the road is a cheer.

Top 10 Countries in the World with the Most Swagger

1. USA
2. Ukraine
3. United Kingdom
4. Switzerland
5. United Arab Emirates
6. France
7. Germany
8. Sweden
9. Japan
10. Singapore

United States has Super Swagger because practically every other country in the world has millions of individuals who would love to live there.

Top 10 Countries in the World with the Least Swagger

1. Russia
2. North Korea
3. Iran
4. Solomon Islands
5. Timor-Leste
6. Bangladesh
7. Belarus
8. Venezuela
9. Rwanda
10. Haiti

To the individual with Super Swagger, there is no significant reason to visit Russia, except for the sheer ecstasy of leaving as quickly as possible.

Top 10 Global Companies with the Most Swagger

1. Apple
2. Tesla
3. BMW
4. Space X
5. Virgin
6. American Express
7. Harley Davidson
8. Starbucks
9. Lululemon
10. The Walt Disney Company

To any person with Swagger, Apple rocks. The New York Times agreed: "Apple served up swaggering advances in technology, year after year, that propelled its business as it became the world's most valuable company."

Top 10 Department Stores in the World with the Most Swagger

1. Harrods, London, England
2. Macy's, New York, USA
3. Le Bon Marché, Paris, France
4. Bloomingdales, New York City, USA
5. Nordstrom, Seattle, USA
6. David Jones, Melbourne, Australia.
7. Beymen, Istanbul, Turkey
8. 9 El Corte Inglés, Barcelona, Madrid, Spain
9. Saks Fifth Avenue, New York, USA
10. Galeries Lafayette, Paris, France

A department store does not have Super Swagger unless it has a room dedicated to expensive chocolate and truffles.

Top 10 Hotels in the World with the Most Swagger

1. Burj Al Arab Jumeirah, Dubai, UAE
2. Soneva Jani, Maldives
3. Bellagio, Las Vegas. Nevada, USA
4. The Plaza, New York, New York, USA
5. Beverly Hills Hotel, Beverly Hills, California, USA
6. Halekulani, Hawaii, USA
7. Claridges Hotel, London, England
8. The Ritz Paris, Paris, France
9. Niyama, Maldives
10. W Barcelona, Barcelona, Spain

Single people with Swagger won't stay in a hotel unless it has a king-size bed in which they can sleep diagonally.

Top 10 Hotel Brands in the World
with the Most Swagger

1. Taj, India
2. Premier Inn
3. Hilton Hotels and Resorts
4. Embassy Suites Hotel
5. JW Marriott
6. Shangri-La Hotels and Resorts
7. Waldorf Astoria Hotels and Resorts
8. W Hotels Worldwide
9. Four Seasons
10. Ritz Carlton

The guy with Raunchy Swagger feels that if he can fit the towels from a hotel in his suitcases that it's worth staying in. Hotels not worth staying in will steal his towel.

Top 10 Haunted Hotels in the US with the Most Swagger

1. Hotel San Carlos, Phoenix, AZ
2. The Hollywood Roosevelt
3. La Fonda on the Plaza, Santa Fe
4. The Stanley Hotel, Colorado
5. Logan Inn, New Hope, PA
6. The Equinox, Vermont
7. Peter Shields Inn, Cape May
8. The Queen Mary, Long Beach, CA
9. Crescent Hotel and Spa, Eureka Springs, AK.
10. Hotel Provincial, New Orleans

The guy with Raunchy Swagger is not afraid of the young woman said to haunt Hotel San Carlos in downtown Phoenix because he knows he can easily scare her away.

Top 10 Radio Stations in the World
with the Most Swagger

1. CKUA — Edmonton, AB, Canada
2. WBGO — New York, NY, USA
3. American Roots — Toronto, ON, Canada
4. NPR (National Public Radio) — USA
5. Soho Radio — London and New York
6. The Lot Radio — New York, NY, USA
7. Radio Paradise
8. Brooklyn Radio — Brooklyn, NY, USA
9. dublab — Los Angeles, Germany, Brazil, Japan, Spain
10. iHeartRadio

BBC Radio 2 would have a lot more Swagger if it played as much great blues music as CKUA's Holger Petersen does.

Top 10 Rock Songs Ever with the Most Swagger

1. *Street Fighting Man* by the Rolling Stones
2. *I Shot the Sheriff* by Bob Marley and the Wailers
3. *Another Brick in the Wall* by Pink Floyd
4. *Won't Get Fooled Again* by The Who
5. *We Will Rock You* by Queen
6. *Leader of the Pack* by The Shangri-Las
7. *Born to Be Wild* by Steppenwolf
8. *Sweet Home Alabama* by Lynyrd Skynyrd
9. *Stairway to Heaven* by Led Zeppelin
10. *Knockin' on Heaven's Door* by Bob Dylan

The singer with Super Swagger may not sing about getting to Heaven but that doesn't mean he or she won't get there.

Top 10 Rock Bands Ever with the Most Swagger

1. Rolling Stones
2. Led Zeppelin
3. Pink Floyd
4. The Who
5. Black Sabbath
6. The Eagles
7. The Beatles
8. Deep Purple
9. Doors
10. Guess Who

Alice Cooper said that "rock music should be arrogant, snotty, and have real Swagger." In this regard, the Rolling Stones had Super Swagger; the Beatles had Elegant Swagger; and Led Zeppelin had Raunchy Swagger.

Top 10 Country Songs Ever with the Most Swagger

1. *It's Hard to Be Humble* by Mac Davis
2. *Put Another Log On The Fire* by Shel Silverstein
3. *Take This Job and Shove It* by Johnny Paycheck
4. *All My Ex's Live in Texas* by George Strait
5. *King of the Road* by Roger Miller
6. *Long Black Veil* by Lefty Frizzell
7. *Sixteen Tons* by Tennessee Ernie Ford
8. *Folsom Prison Blues* by Johnny Cash
9. *Okie from Muskogee* by Merle Haggard
10. *The Happiest Girl in the Whole U.S.A* by Donna Fargo

The character with Raunchy Swagger loves country music because it's real music that many pretentious blowhards laugh at but can't understand.

Top 10 Country and Western Band "Names" Ever with the Most Swagger

1. Cement City Cowboys
2. Ozark Mountain Daredevils
3. Pistol Annies
4. The Highwaymen
5. The Mavericks
6. The Flying Burrito Brothers
7. Florida Georgia Line
8. Nitty Gritty Dirt Band
9. Drive-By Truckers
10. Asleep at the Wheel

People with Elegant Swagger like Country and Western music as much as they like Classical and Jazz.

Top 10 Rock Albums Ever with the Most Swagger

1. *Bat Out of Hell* by Meat Loaf
2. *The Wall* by Pink Floyd
3. *Appetite For Destruction* by Guns N' Roses
4. *Physical Graffiti* by Led Zeppelin
5. *Legend* by Bob Marley & The Wailers
6. *Hotel California* by the Eagles
7. *The White Album* by The Beatles
8. *Back In Black* by AC/DC
9. *Rumours* by Fleetwood Mac
10. *Thriller* by Michael Jackson

The guy with Raunchy Swagger lets his neighbors listen to his favorite blues and rock music on his super stereo for free without the neighbors having to visit him.

Top 10 Blues Albums Ever with the Most Swagger

1. *King Of The Delta Blues* by Robert Johnson
2. *Born Under A Bad Sign* by Albert King
3. *I Am The Blues* by Willie Dixon
4. *A Man and The Blues* by Buddy Guy
5. *Moanin' In The Moonlight* by Howlin' Wolf
6. *Coffee Blues* by Mississippi John Hurt
7. *The Natch'l Blues* by Taj Mahal
8. *Blues After Hours* by Elmore James
9. *I Do Not Play No Rock and Roll* by Mississippi Fred McDowell
10. *Down and Out Blues* by Sonny Boy Williamson

The Swagger character with any knowledge of the blues agrees with Willie Dixon: "The blues are the roots [of all American music] and the other musics are the fruits."

Top 10 YouTube Music Videos Ever
with the Most Swagger

1. *Copperhead Road* by Steve Earle
2. *Rock n Roll Music* by Tina Turner & Chuck Berry
3. *Whole Lot of Shaking Going On* by Jerry Lee Lewis
4. *Statesboro Blues* by Taj Mahal and Ry Cooder
5. *Bat out of Hell* by Meat Loaf
6. *November Rain* by Guns N' Roses
7. *It's My Life* by Bon Jovi
8. *Wagon Wheel* by the Old Crow Medicine Show
9. *Can't You See* by Toy Caldwell and the Marshall Tucker Band
10. *Me and Bobby McGee* by The Highwaymen

*The individual with Elegant Swagger does not listen to rap
music when listening to classical is an option.*

Top 10 Blues Guitarists Ever
with the Most Swagger

1. Stevie Ray Vaughan
2. BB King
3. Buddy Guy
4. Albert King
5. Joe Bonamassa
6. Robert Johnson
7. Rory Gallagher
8. Muddy Waters
9. Kenny Wayne Shepherd
10. Bonnie Rait

Swagger guitarist Keith Richards was right: "If you don't know the blues, there's no point in picking up the guitar and playing rock and roll or any other form of popular music."

Top 10 Rock Guitarists Ever
with the Most Swagger

1. Jimmy Hendrik
2. Stevie Ray Vaughan
3. Jimmy Page
4. Keith Richards
5. Jeff Beck
6. Chuck Berry
7. Carlos Santana
8. Frank Zappa
9. Pete Townshend
10. Ry Cooder

Achievers with Elegant Swagger know that there will never be another Jimmy Hendrik. Of course, there won't be another Stevie Ray Vaughan either.

Top 10 Blues Singers Ever with the Most Swagger

1. Bessie Smith
2. Etta James
3. Muddy Waters
4. Howlin' Wolf
5. Billie Holiday
6. B.B. King
7. Jimmy Rushing
8. Ma Rainey
9. Bobby "Blue" Bland
10. Big Mama Thornton

*The individual with Raunchy Swagger angrily sings the
blues when having to listen to rap.*

Top 10 Blues Songs Ever with the Most Swagger

1. *'Taint Nobody's Bizness If I Do* by Bessie Smith
2. *(I'm Your) Hoochie Coochie Man* by Muddy Waters
3. *Hell Hound On My Trail* by Robert Johnson
4. *Statesboro Blues* by Taj Mahal
5. *See That My Grave Is Kept Clean* by Blind Lemon Jefferson
6. *Baby Scratch My Back* by Slim Harpo
7. *Give Me Back My Wig* by Hound Dog Taylor
8. *Devil Got My Woman* by Skip James
9. *Rock Me Mama* by Arthur 'Big Boy' Crudup
10. *Born to Play Guitar* by Buddy Guy

*There is a bit of Swagger in all blues music that does its
listeners a measure of good and that they can relate to.*

Top 10 Jazz Musicians Ever with the Most Swagger

1. Duke Ellington
2. Louis Armstrong
3. Thelonious Monk
4. Miles Davis
5. Dizzy Gilliespie
6. Billie Holliday
7. Charlie Parker
8. Ella Fitzgerald
9. Charlie Mingus
10. Lester Young

American dancer Isadora Duncan stated, "It seems to me monstrous that anyone should believe that the jazz rhythm expresses America. Jazz rhythm expresses the primitive savage." The person with Swagger feels this better reflects rap.

Top 10 Female Singers Ever
with the Most Swagger

1. Tina Turner
2. Janis Choplin
3. Stevie Nicks
4. Dianna Ross
5. Ariana Grande
6. Taylor Swift
7. Mariah Carey
8. Beyoncé
9. Madonna
10. Lady Gaga

With her Swagger, Tina Turner proved that music produces a sensational enjoyment that humans cannot do without.

Top 10 Male Singers Ever with the Most Swagger

1. Mick Jagger
2. Chuck Berry
3. Jerry Lee Lewis
4. Elton John
5. David Bowie
6. Prince
7. Bruce Springsteen
8. Elvis Presley
9. Julio José Iglesias
10. Tom Jones

Einstein said, "If I were not a physicist, I would probably be a musician." No doubt he would have been a great musician but he wouldn't have had as much Swagger as Mick Jagger.

Top 10 Artists Ever with the Most Swagger

1. Pablo Picasso
2. Pierre-Auguste Renoir
3. Leonardo da Vinci
4. Rembrandt
5. Michelangelo
6. Salvador Dali
7. Vincent Van Gogh
8. Claude Monet
9. Edvard Munch
10. Henri Matisse

Picasso during one of his Swaggerific moments proclaimed, "Disciples be damned. It's not interesting. It's only the masters that matter. Those who create."

Top 10 Paintings Ever with the Most Swagger

1. 'Mona Lisa' by Leonardo da Vinci
2. 'The Last Supper' by Leonardo da Vinci
3. 'Guernica' by Picasso
4. 'The Starry Night' by Vincent van Gogh
5. 'Three Musicians' by Picasso
6. 'The Scream' by Edvard Munch
7. 'The Persistence of Memory' by Salvador Dali
8. 'The Kiss' by Gustav Klimt
9. 'Girl With a Pearl Earring' by Johannes Vermeer
10. 'The Birth of Venus' by Sandro Botticelli

The moment you declare that a particular work of art has Swagger, the blowhard elitist artist will tell you that you have no idea what you are talking about.

Top 10 American Professions with the Most Swagger

1. Doctor
2. Firefighter
3. Airplane Pilot
4. Engineer
5. Police Swat Team
6. Registered Nurse
7. Entrepreneur
8. Teacher
9. Ambulance worker
10. Private Investigator

The doctor with Elegant Swagger prescribes the least number of medicines and at the same time encourages the doctor within the patient to do the healing.

Top 10 American Professions
with the Least Swagger

1. Politician in Congress
2. Used Car Salesperson
3. Advertising Professional
4. State Officeholder
5. Government Worker
6. Real Estate Salesperson
7. Pig Farmer
8. Ditch Digger with an Engineering Degree
9. Artist/Author
10. Entertainer

The intelligent person with Swagger knows that when most politicians come up with a new idea it will be a magnet for disaster if implemented. It will also cost a lot of money.

Top 10 American Trade Professions
with the Most Swagger

1. Ironworker
2. Lumberjack
3. Firefighter
4. Electrician
5. Welder
6. Oil Rig Driller
7. Plumber
8. Machinist
9. Boilermaker
10. Heavy Duty Mechanic

Super achievers with Swagger going into the trades choose one in which they can earn more than the average doctor.

Top 10 World Professions with the Most Swagger

1. Doctor
2. Lawyer
3. Engineer
4. Head Teacher
5. Police Officer
6. Nurse
7. Accountant
8. Local Government Manager
9. Management Consultant
10. Secondary School Teacher

The doctor with Super Swagger is confident in his or her abilities but nevertheless realizes that science does not have all the answers to health and healing.

Top 10 Jobs with the Least Swagger Once Performed by Famous People

1. Grave Digger performed by Rod Stewart
2. Dishwasher performed by Warren Beatty
3. Manure Shoveller in Horse Stables performed by Jerry Hall
4. Dog Kennel Cleaner performed by Cyndi Lauper
5. Coffin Polisher performed by Sean Connery
6. Makeup Artist for Corpses performed by Whoopi Goldberg
7. Giant Chicken Impersonator performed by Brad Pitt
8. Fuller Brush Salesman performed by Pee-Wee Herman
9. Milkman performed by Benny Hill
10. Encyclopedia Salesman performed by Frank Zappa

Super achievers with Swagger do not dig ditches or make love as their flagship career.

Top 10 Men's Names Ever with the Most Swagger

1. Rocco
2. Attila
3. Ivan
4. Napoleon
5. Benjamin
6. Malcolm
7. Winston
8. Oscar
9. Brock
10. Anthony

The inheritance of a name with Swagger is a noble
inheritance to the individual who does the name proud.

Top 10 Women's Names Ever
with the Most Swagger

1. Cleopatra
2. Athena
3. Alexandria
4. Marilyn
5. Catherine
6. Cassandra
7. Sabina
8. Godiva
9. Nikita
10. Thora

*A woman's name with Swagger will make a guy's knees
weak when he first hears it.*

Top 10 Real Names with Swagger That Sound Like Stage Names

1. Humphrey Bogart
2. Marlo Brando
3. Clint Eastwood
4. Marianne Faithfull
5. Clark Gable
6. Dustin Hoffman
7. Dolly Parton
8. Kris Kristofferson
9. Olivia de Havilland
10. Elvis Presley

Whenever a bloke with Raunchy Swagger is asked, "Is that your real name?" he sarcastically replies, "No, I am just breaking it in for a friend."

Top 10 Cat Names with the Most Swagger

1. Spike
2. Tiger
3. Blackie
4. Thor
5. Max
6. Brutus
7. Bandit
8. Lion
9. Napoleon
10. Magnum Warrior

The cat with Swagger will always wind up with his favorite place on the sofa even if three pit bulls live in the house.

Top 10 Dog Names with the Most Swagger

1. Trooper
2. Butch
3. Rocky
4. Torch
5. Bear
6. Rambo
7. Gunner
8. Bruiser
9. Crusher
10. Hurricane

The guy with Raunchy Swagger who has teenage children owns a Swaggerific dog so that someone in the house is happy to see him when he gets home.

Top 10 Cartoon Strips Ever with the Most Swagger

1. *Calvin and Hobbes* by Bill Watterson
2. *The Far Side* by Gary Larson
3. *Dilbert* by Scott Adams
4. *Bizarro* by Dan Piraro
5. *Herman* by Jim Unger
6. *Mr. Boffo* by Joe Martin
7. *Andy Capp* by Reg Smythe
8. *Garfield* by Jim Davis
9. *Life in Hell* by Matt Groening
10. *Peanuts* by Charles Schulz

The person with Elegant Swagger loves Calvin and Hobbes
most because creator Bill Watterson turned down hundreds
of millions of dollars to have it merchandised.

Top 10 Financial Gurus with the Most Swagger

1. Kevin O'Leary
2. Jim Cramer
3. Larry Winget
4. Suze Orman
5. Robert Kiyosaki
6. Peter Lynch
7. Dave Ramsey
8. Ben Stein
9. Mark Cuban
10. Charles Ponzi

Kevin O'Leary is able to display Super Swagger when he holds a copy of the international bestseller "How to Retire Happy, Wild, and Free" instead of a book written by him.

Top 10 Metals in the World with the Most Swagger

1. Gold
2. Platinum
3. Silver
4. Rhodium
5. Iridium
6. Palladium
7. Rhenium
8. Ruthenium
9. Osmium
10. Scandium

Gold has the most Swagger because everywhere in the world
it will always open doors that other metals won't.

Top 10 Gold Coins with the Most Swagger

1. South African Krugerrand
2. American Buffalo
3. Canadian Maple Leaf
4. United Kingdom Britannia
5. Mexican Centenario
6. Israel Jerusalem of Gold Series
7. Austrian Vienna Philharmonic
8. American Gold Eagle
9. Ukraine Archangel Michael
10. Isle of Man Angel

Silver coins may shine but Gold coins have Swagger
because they will never ever give up their luster.

Top 10 World Currencies with the Most Swagger

1. US Dollar
2. Euro
3. British Pound
4. Swiss Franc
5. Cayman Islands Dollar
6. Kuwaiti Dinar
7. Bahraini Dinar
8. Omani Rial
9. Jordanian Dinar
10. Bermudian Dollar

The character with Super Swagger at one time thought that the Singapore currency had the most Swagger because until lately one could get a Singapore $10,000 bill.

Top 10 Earth's Mountain Ranges
with the Most Swagger

1. Rocky Mountains
2. Alps
3. Atlas Mountains
4. Himalayas
5. Andes
6. Ethiopian Highlands
7. Great Dividing Range
8. Transantarctic Mountains
9. Ural Mountains
10. Appalachian Mountains

Ordinary individuals stumble over pebbles; extraordinary individuals with Swagger stumble over mountains.

Top 10 Mountains in the World with the Most Swagger

1. Mount Everest, border between Nepal and Tibet
2. Matterhorn, border between Switzerland and Italy
3. K2, border between China and Pakistan
4. Mount Assiniboine, Canada
5. Mount Kailash, Tibet
6. Mount Fitz Roy, border between Argentina and Chile
7. Aoraki/Mount Cook, New Zealand
8. Kilimanjaro, Tanzania, Africa
9. Vinicunca, Peru
10. Denali, USA

Dreamers who are not doers climb an imaginary mountain because it isn't there. People with Swagger who are doers climb a real mountain because it's there.

Top 10 Rivers in the World with the Most Swagger

1. Zambezi
2. Amazon
3. Nile
4. Yangtze
5. Mississippi
6. Yenisei
7. Yellow
8. Danube
9. Ganges
10. Ob-Irtysh

*The mightiest river in the world to the individual with Super
Swagger is the one that is most dangerous to swim across.*

Top 10 Bridges in the World with the Most Swagger

1. Golden Gate Bridge, San Francisco, US
2. Tower Bridge, London, England
3. Sydney Harbour Bridge, Sydney, Australia
4. Ponte Vecchio, Florence, Italy
5. Brooklyn Bridge, New York, US
6. Tsing Ma Bridge, Hong Kong, China
7. Charles Bridge, Prague, Czechia
8. Gateshead Millennium Bridge: Gateshead, England
9. Rialto Bridge, Venice, Italy
10. Akashi-Kaikyo Bridge, Kobe, Japan

Individuals with Swagger sometimes have to burn a few
bridges to prevent the crazies from following them.

Top 10 Plants in the World with the Most Swagger

1. Deadly Nightshade (Atropa belladonna)
2. Thornapples (Datura genus)
3. Monkshood, wolf's bane, etc (Aconitum genus)
4. Hemlock water-dropwort (Oenanthe crocata)
5. Cerbera odollam (colloquial name "suicide tree")
6. Rosary Pea, or crab's eye vine (Abrus precatorius)
7. Oleander (Nerium oleander)
8. Lily-Of-The-Valley (Convallaria majalis)
9. Manchineel (Hippomane mancinella)
10. Tobacco (Nicotiana tabacum)

The individual with Raunchy Swagger likes to quip to waiters at vegetarian restaurants, "I am thinking of becoming a fulltime vegetarian. You may think that it's because I love animals — not so, it's because I hate plants."

Top 10 Tree Species in the World
with the Most Swagger

1. Coast Redwood (Sequoia Sempervirens)
2. Yellow Meranti (Shorea Faguetiana)
3. Mountain Ash (Eucalyptus Regnans)
4. Coast Douglas-Fir (Pseudotsuga Menziesii var. Menziesii)
5. Sitka Spruce (Picea Sitchensis)
6. Giant Sequoia (Sequoiadendron Giganteum)
7. Manna Gum (Eucalyptus Viminalis)
8. Southern Blue Gum (Eucalyptus Globulus)
9. Noble Fir (Abies Procera)
10. Dinizia Excelsa

Characters with Super Swagger feel that a tree with up to a diameter of 30 feet such as the Coast Redwood is worth hugging and talking about.

Top 10 Individual Trees in the World Ever with the Most Swagger

1. Tree of Ténéré, Sahara Desert, Niger
2. The Ashbrittle Yew, Ashbrittle, United Kingdom
3. General Sherman in California's Sequoia National Park
4. The Jaya Sri Maha Bodhi, Sri Lanka
5. Anne Frank's Tree
6. Hyperion
7. 9/11 Survivor Tree
8. The Running Tree, Maui, Hawaii, USA
9. Old Tjikko
10. El Arbol Del Tule

Solitary trees with Swagger grow strong, prosperous, and free until a drunken Libyan truck driver knocks them down like happened to the Tree of Ténéré in the Sahara Desert.

Top 10 Mountain Bike Brands with the Most Swagger

1. Rocky Mountain, Vancouver, B.C.
2. Evil Bike Co., Bellingham, Washington
3. Yeti Cycles, Golden, Colorado
4. Santa Cruz, Santa Cruz, California
5. Specialized, Morgan Hill, California
6. Trek Bikes, Waterloo, Wisconsin
7. Pivot Cycles, Tempe, Arizona
8. Giant Bicycles, Taichung, Taiwan
9. Cannondale, Wilton, Connecticut
10. Kona, Ferndale, Washington

Achievers with Swagger do not ride a bicycle without hands on the handlebars on busy city streets. That's what suicidal maniacs do for attention. They also don't ride eBikes.

Top 10 Non-Fiction Book Titles Ever with the Most Swagger

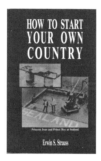

1. *How to Start Your Own Country* by Erwin S. Strauss
2. *How to Disappear Completely and Never be Found* by Doug Richmond
3. *How to Write While You Sleep* by Elizabeth Irwin Ross
4. *Be Your Own Undertaker* by A.R. Bowman
5. *How to Argue and Win Every Time* by Gerry L. Spence
6. *101 Things to Do 'Til the Revolution* by Claire Wolfe
7. *Reinventing Anarchy, Again* by Howard J. Ehrilch
8. *Do-it-yourself Coffins for Pets and People* by Dale Power
9. *How to Beat Honesty Tests* by Pete Sneaky
10. *How to Hide Things in Public Places* by Dennis Fiery

Individuals with Super Swagger buy a lot of great books — even if they never read all of them.

Top 10 Books about Money Ever with the Most Swagger

1. *You Are a Badass at Making Money* by Jen Sincero
2. *The Lazy Man's Guide to Riches* by Joe Karbo
3. *You're Broke Because You Want to Be* by Larry Winget
4. *Million Dollar Habits* by Robert J. Ringer
5. *Think and Grow Rich* by Napoleon Hill
6. *Secrets of the Millionaire Mind* by T. Harv Eker
7. *The Science of Getting Rich* by Wallace D. Wattles
8. *The Richest Man in Babylon* by George S. Clason
9. *Money Madness* by Henry Goldberg and Robert T. Lewis
10. *Rich Dad, Poor Dad* by Robert T. Kiyosaki

If achievers with Swagger can't boast about knowing something important about money, they boast about not knowing something important about money.

Top 10 Authors of Money Books
with the Most Swagger

1. Jen Sincero, *You Are a Badass at Making Money*
2. Kevin O'Leary, *Cold Hard Truth on Men, Women & Money*
3. Larry Winget, *You're Broke Because You Want to Be*
4. Robert J. Ringer, *Million Dollar Habits*
5. David Bach, *The Automatic Millionaire*
6. Suze Orman, *The 9 Steps to Financial Freedom*
7. T. Harv Eker, *Secrets of the Millionaire Mind*
8. Vicki Robin, *Your Money or Your Life*
9. Napoleon Hill, *Think and Grow Rich*
10. David Chilton, *The Wealthy Barber*

*Swagger authors of books about money keep buying books
about money even when they are financially independent
themselves. They realize that they don't know everything.*

Top 10 Songs with the Most Swagger to Have Played at Your Funeral or Memorial Service

1. *Stairway to Heaven* by Led Zeppelin
2. *Knockin' On Heaven's Door* by Bob Dylan
3. *[I Can't Get No] Satisfaction* by The Rolling Stones
4. *I'm Gone* by Rick Holmstrom
5. *If The Phone Doesn't Ring, It's Me* by Jimmy Buffet
6. *If You Wanna Get to Heaven, (You Got to Raise a Little Hell)* by Ozark Mountain Daredevils
7. *I Still Haven't Found What I Have Been Looking For* by U2
8. *I Didn't Come Here (And I Ain't Leavin')* by Willie Nelson
9. *Prop Me Up Beside The Jukebox (If I Die)* by Joe Diffie
10. *Sneakin' Into Heaven* by The California Honeydrops

To have been born with Swagger is an accident. To die with Swagger is a remarkable achievement!

About the Author

Ernie J. Zelinski has been a ditch digger, a wheel barrow pilot, an equipment operator, a laborer, a flag man, an electrical engineer, a college instructor, a professional speaker, and an international best-selling author. Ernie spends a lot of his vacation time in Vancouver, BC; New York, NY; London, England; and Honolulu, Hawaii. You may see him on his daily morning runs near Stanley Park in Vancouver, in Central Park in New York, in Battersea Park in London, or in Ala Moana Park in Honolulu.

One of Ernie's biggest Swagger moves was to ditch his engineering career so that he could attain personal freedom and financial independence by being self-employed and only work four to five hours a day. Although he is generally lazy, he still has a Type A personality. He always brings his A-game and Swagger to his important projects so that he can pulverize the competition.

Ernie doesn't like sitting in the cheap seats on airplanes, the symphony, live theater, or at Rolling Stones concerts. His favorite wines are Mollydooker The Boxer Shiraz and Mollydooker Blue Eyed Boy Shiraz. If enough people buy this book, he intends to regularly drink the much more expensive 1982 Chateau Latour. He may also hire a butler. Ernie J. Zelinski has lived and continues to live by the adage, "Be a Learner first, a Master second, and a Student always."

Contact Ernie at vipbooks@telus.net or Ph. 780-434-9202.

The Little Black Book of Swagger
637 Swagger Tips for Super Achievers

Available at Amazon.com and Fine Bookstores throughout the Universe

"This Zelinski guy knows how to write prose that has the potential to become those old proverbs everyone repeats."
— Herb Denenberg, *Philadelphia Evening Bulletin*

"If you can't find it in the Bible, you will find it in Shakespeare. And if you can't find it in Shakespeare, you will find it in Zelinski."
— Modern day saying

"Stronger than an army is a book whose time has come. Although the author runs me down somewhere inside this tome, this book rocks. It's simply Swaggerific. Even Shake would envy this Masterpiece."
— Donald J. Tramp